People Who Predict

Estimating

Diana Noonan

Publishing Credits

Editor
Sara Johnson

Editorial Director
Emily R. Smith, M.A.Ed.

Editor-in-Chief
Sharon Coan, M.S.Ed.

Creative Director
Lee Aucoin

Publisher
Rachelle Cracchiolo, M.S.Ed.

Image Credits

The author and publisher would like to gratefully credit or acknowledge the following for permission to reproduce copyright material: cover, Big Stock Photos; p.1, Photodisc; p.4 (below), Photodisc; p.4 (above), Shutterstock; p.6, Photodisc; p.7, Corbis; p.8, Big Stock Photos; p.9, Elvele Images/Alamy; p.10, Corbis; p.11, Kevin Foy/Alamy; p.12, Jochen Tack/Alamy; p.13, Corbis; p.14, Visions of America, LLC/Alamy; p.15, Visions of America, LLC/Alamy; p.16, I Stock Photos; p.17, NYCFoto.com; p.18, Shutterstock; p.19, NYCFoto.com; p.20, Corbis; p.21, Stock Connection Blue/Alamy; p.22, Getty Images; p.23, Alex Segre/Alamy; p.24 (left), Photodisc; p.24 (right), Ken Welsh/Alamy; p.25, Alice McBroom; p.26 (above), Photodisc; p.26 (below left), Shutterstock; p.26 (below right), Big Stock Photos; p.27 (above), Big Stock Photos; p.27 (below right), Shutterstock; p.27 (below left), Corbis RF; p.29, Big Stock Photos

While every care has been taken to trace and acknowledge copyright, the publishers tender their apologies for any accidental infringement where copyright has proved untraceable. They would be pleased to come to a suitable arrangement with the rightful owner in each case.

Teacher Created Materials

5301 Oceanus Drive
Huntington Beach, CA 92649-1030
http://www.tcmpub.com
ISBN 978-0-7439-0906-8
© 2009 Teacher Created Materials, Inc.
Made in China
Nordica.032016.CA21600284

Table of Contents

Natural Disasters

Natural disasters can happen at any time. They might be tornadoes, **tsunamis** (soo-NAHM-eez), or **volcanic eruptions**. So it's good to be prepared. **Predictions** can help prepare us for disasters.

Data

Scientists collect and use data. Data helps them make predictions. They share the data and their predictions with other experts.

LET'S EXPLORE MATH

Millions of tiny earthquakes happen each year in the world. Most are so small, you cannot feel them. Many happen in **remote** places.

Yearly Earthquakes in the United States

Year	2005	2006	2007
Number of earthquakes	3,685	2,783	2,791

a. Round each number to the nearest 1,000. **Estimate** the total number of earthquakes.

b. Round each number to the nearest 100. Estimate the total number of earthquakes.

c. Compare the 2 estimates. Which do you think is more accurate?

Volcanologists

Volcanologists (VOL-kuh-NOWL-uh-jists) learn about volcanoes. They try to predict if and when a volcano will erupt. But these predictions can be very hard to make.

A volcanologist at work

Global Positioning System (GPS)

Volcanologists use **GPS** technology. It helps them predict eruptions. Satellites send signals to equipment set up on a volcano. Graphs record the changing shape of a volcano. This is a clue to whether it may erupt.

Tiltmeters

Volcanologists use **tiltmeters**. When a volcano is likely to erupt, its sides move up and out. A tiltmeter measures any tilt in the volcano slope. Tilting can be a sign that the volcano may erupt.

A tiltmeter

Seismometers

Volcanologists also use **seismometers** (size-MAWM-uh-tuhrs) to help with predictions. Seismometers measure movements in the earth. **Molten** (MOHL-tuhn) rock moves inside volcanoes. Seismometers record any earthquakes caused by this.

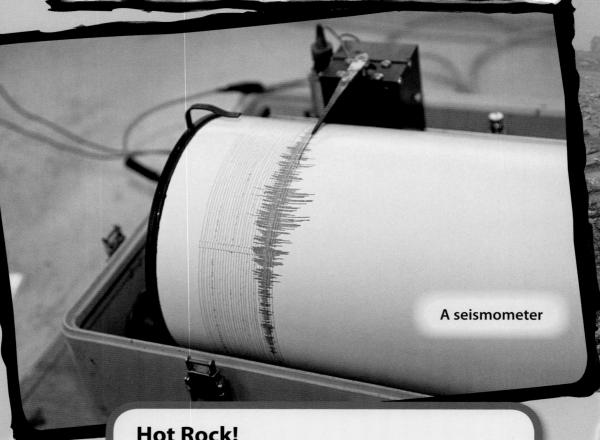

A seismometer

Hot Rock!

Magma is molten rock under Earth's surface. When a volcano erupts, the magma is forced to the surface. It becomes lava.

Testing for Gas

Volcanoes give off gases. Volcanologists test these gases. Changes in the gases could mean a volcano may soon erupt.

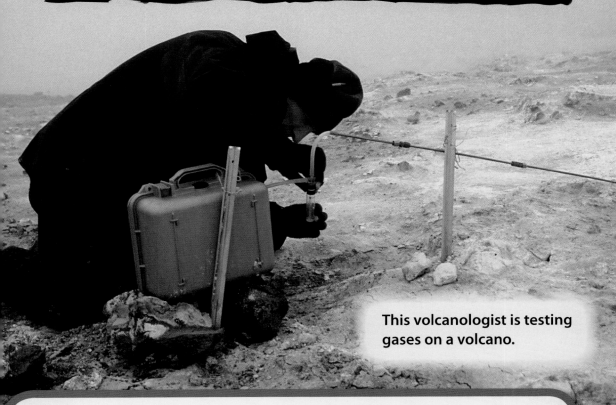

This volcanologist is testing gases on a volcano.

Volcanic Islands

Hawaii has many volcanoes. This graph shows the heights of 3 of its volcanoes.

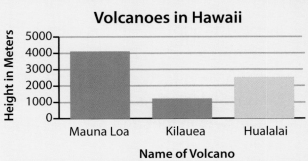

Volcanoes in Hawaii

Height in Meters: 5000, 4000, 3000, 2000, 1000, 0

Name of Volcano: Mauna Loa, Kilauea, Hualalai

Predictions Are Hard!

But the data from these instruments is not always helpful to volcanologists. Some eruptions just cannot be predicted.

Mount St. Helens erupting

LET'S EXPLORE MATH

In 1980, Mount St. Helens erupted. Before the eruption, its height was 9,677 feet (2,950 m). Today, its height is 8,363 feet (2,549 m). Estimate how much smaller Mount St. Helens is today than before it erupted. Give the answer in feet and meters. *Hint*: Use rounding to the nearest 100 and subtraction to help you.

Preparing for Disaster

Volcanologists try to predict if a volcano will erupt. Then they tell other experts. These experts try to guess what **damage** may happen to any towns near the volcano.

A town destroyed by a volcanic eruption

Planners

Planners are experts that work with volcanologists. Planners choose the best routes people should use if they need to leave their towns. They also help decide when it is safe for these people to go back to their homes.

Seismologists

Seismologists (size-MAWL-uh-jists) study earthquakes. They predict where big earthquakes may occur.

This seismologist is measuring the movements on a seismometer.

Measuring Earthquakes

Earthquakes cause **tremors** in the earth. These tremors are measured on a scale called the Richter (RIK-tuhr) scale. An earthquake measuring less than 3.5 on the Richter scale is not usually felt by people. An earthquake measuring 6.0 or greater can cause serious damage.

Seismologists also use seismometers. Some seismometers measure the smallest earthquakes. Others measure larger earthquakes. Graphs record these movements.

This table shows the number of earthquakes in the world per year measuring between 3.0 and 3.9 on the Richter scale. Use the table to answer the questions below. *Hint:* Use rounding to the nearest 100 to help you with your answers.

Year	2003	2004	2005	2006	2007
Number of earthquakes	7,624	7,932	9,191	9,990	9,889

a. About how many earthquakes were there in 2003 and 2004?

b. About how many earthquakes were there in 2005, 2006, and 2007?

c. About how many earthquakes does this chart show altogether?

Creepmeters

Seismologists also learn about very small, slow earth movements. They use **creepmeters** to do this. Creepmeters help seismologists predict when a big change is on its way.

Creepmeters are buried in the earth.

Predicting an Earthquake

It is not easy for seismologists to predict when earthquakes will happen. But collecting data can help. Changes in small earth movements may help seismologists predict big earthquakes.

This seismologist is reading the data made by a seismometer.

LET'S EXPLORE MATH

This table shows the number of earthquakes recorded each year.

a. Round each number to the nearest 1,000.

b. Estimate about how many more earthquakes there were in 2006 than in 2000.

c. Predict how many earthquakes you think will be recorded in 2010. Explain your prediction.

Earthquakes Recorded

Year	Number
2006	29,568
2005	30,478
2004	31,194
2003	31,419
2002	27,453
2001	23,665
2000	22,256

Planners

Seismologists also track how many big earthquakes have hit one place. Then they divide the number of earthquakes by the number of years between earthquakes.

There have been many earthquakes in San Francisco.

Earthquakes in San Francisco

This table shows earthquakes in San Francisco that measured greater than 6.0 on the Richter scale.

Year	Richter Scale Measurement
1892	6.5
1898	6.5
1906	8.2
1911	6.5
1989	6.9

Seismologists tell planners where they think a big earthquake may happen. Planners can then help towns prepare for disasters.

Buildings and Roads

Buildings and roads can break during an earthquake. Experts need to figure out how to build them so this will not happen. Experts from Japan are world leaders in this kind of work.

Being Prepared

People must be prepared for earthquakes. Many homes and offices have earthquake kits. First aid kits, food, and water can help people **survive**.

These Filipino students are practicing an earthquake drill.

Earthquake Drills

Students and office staff who live in earthquake areas have regular earthquake drills.

Meteorologists

Meteorologists (mee-tee-uh-ROL-uh-jists) study weather data. They use the data to make weather **forecasts**. They also predict natural disasters. They can warn people about tornadoes or hurricanes.

A meteorologist measuring wind speed

LET'S EXPLORE MATH

This table shows the number of tornadoes in the United States from 2005 to 2007.

Year	Number of Tornadoes
2007	1,093
2006	1,106
2005	1,264

a. Round each number to the nearest 100.

b. Estimate the total number of tornadoes for these 3 years.

Weather Stations

Many meteorologists work at weather stations. Weather stations collect weather data, such as air temperature. They also collect weather data on wind speed and air pressure. Meteorologists from all around the world use this data to make forecasts.

Barometers

Barometers measure change in air pressure. Hurricanes and other storms often begin in areas of low air pressure. Barometers are very helpful in weather predictions.

Rain Records

Meteorologists use rain gauges to check how much rain has fallen. Some of these gauges are in very remote places. These rain gauges use satellites to send the data to weather stations.

A meteorologist using a rain gauge

Meteosats

Meteorological satellites are known as meteosats. They send pictures of Earth to weather stations. Meteosats can record cloud patterns. They quickly show where big storms are forming.

This image shows the path of Hurricane Katrina.

Satellite Tracking

Meteosats help track the course of hurricanes. Predictions can be made about where a disaster is likely to happen.

Doppler Radars

Doppler radars help meteorologists predict tornadoes. Doppler radars are set up all over the United States. They collect data on the direction and speed of winds.

A Doppler radar on a truck

Fire

Meteorologists can also predict very dry, hot weather. Firefighters use the weather forecasts to prepare for fires. When it is very dry, people are warned not to light fires outdoors.

Forest Fires

Firefighters use data on wind direction and air temperature. This data helps them decide where to place fire crews.

Predict and Prepare

On August 29, 2005, Hurricane Katrina hit the city of New Orleans. Meteorologists had predicted its arrival. The city was warned and people were told to leave. Thousands of lives were saved.

LET'S EXPLORE MATH

This table shows 4 powerful hurricanes. These hurricanes all hit land in the southeastern United States.

Hurricane	Wind Speed on Land (miles per hour)
Katrina	125
Andrew	165
Camille	190
Florida Keys	200

Round each numbers to the nearest 10. Estimate the average speed of all the hurricanes.

The result of Hurricane Katrina

Past, Present, and Future

Weather data from the past can help weather predictions for the future. Many scientists believe that Earth's climate is growing warmer. Some meteorologists predict that storms will become more serious in the future.

The city of New Orleans after Hurricane Katrina

Natural disasters are part of our world. But thanks to people who predict, we can be better prepared for them. Being prepared means that lives can be saved.

A meterologist tracking a hurricane

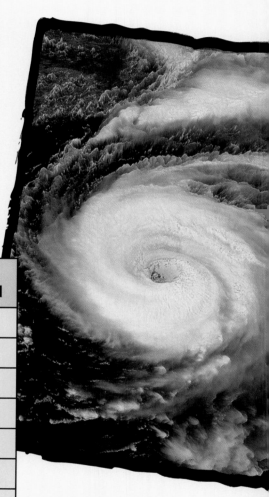

Windyville Evacuated!

Scientists have been studying the number of hurricanes in Windyville over the past 8 years. They have also collected data on the number of people that needed evacuation. This table shows their data.

Hurricane Evacuations

Year	Hurricanes	People Evacuated
2007	5	1,195
2006	3	823
2005	4	1,072
2004	2	586
2003	0	0
2002	1	217
2001	2	503
2000	1	195

Solve It!

Estimate how many people were evacuated:

a. from 2000 to 2003.

b. from 2004 to 2007.

c. over the 8 years.

Use the steps below to help you solve these problems.

Step 1: Round to the nearest 100 the number of people evacuated each year.

Step 2: Add the numbers to find the total number of people evacuated from 2000 to 2003.

Step 3: Add the numbers to find the total number of people evacuated from 2004 to 2007.

Step 4: Add your answers together to work out the answer to **c.**

Glossary

creepmeters—instruments that measure movements of a geological fault line

damage—harm done to a person or thing

Doppler radars—instruments that can measure the direction and speed of winds

estimate—to make a rough calculation or guess

forecasts—predictions of what will happen in the future

Global Positioning System (GPS)—a system that uses satellites orbiting Earth to provide data about objects on Earth

meteorological—to do with the study of climate and weather

meteorologists—people who study climate and weather

molten—turned into liquid by heat

natural disasters—events occuring in nature, such as tornadoes or floods, that cause huge amounts of damage

predictions—acts of predicting; having said in advance that something will happen

remote—far away, out of the way from other places

seismologists—people who study earthquakes and vibrations in the earth

seismometers—instruments that measure movements in the ground

survive—to continue to live after a certain event

tiltmeters—instruments that measure the tilting of Earth's surface

tremors—shakes or vibrations of Earth, especially before or after a major earthquake

tsunamis—large ocean waves made by earthquakes or underwater landslides

volcanic eruptions—when lava and molten rocks burst out of volcanoes

volcanologists—people who study volcanoes

Index

Let's Explore Math

Page 5:
a. 4,000 + 3,000 + 3,000 = 10,000 earthquakes
b. 3,700 + 2,800 + 2,800 = 9,300 earthquakes
c. Answers may vary. Rounding to the nearest 100 is more accurate than rounding to the nearest 1,000 because the total is closer to the actual amount.

Page 10:
9,700 feet – 8,400 feet = 1,300 feet smaller in height
(3,000 m – 2,600 m = 400 m)

Page 13:
a. 7,600 + 7,900 = 15,500 earthquakes
b. 9,200 + 10,000 + 9,900 = 29,100 earthquakes
c. About 44,000 earthquakes altogether

Page 15:
a. **Earthquakes Recorded**

Year	Number
2006	30,000
2005	30,000
2004	31,000
2003	31,000
2002	27,000
2001	24,000
2000	22,000

b. There were approximately 8,000 more recorded earthquakes.
c. Answers will vary.

Page 19:
a.

Year	Number of Tornadoes
2007	1,100
2006	1,100
2005	1,300

b. 3,500 tornadoes

Page 25:
130 + 170 + 190 + 200 = 690 miles per hour
690 ÷ 4 = 172.5 miles per hour

Problem-Solving Activity

Step 1:

Year	Hurricanes	People Evacuated
2007	5	1,200
2006	3	800
2005	4	1,100
2004	2	600
2003	0	0
2002	1	200
2001	2	500
2000	1	200

a. Approximately 900 people were evacuated from 2000 to 2003.
b. Approximately 3,700 people were evacuated from 2004 to 2007.
c. Approximately 4,600 people were evacuated over the 8 years.